THE SORROW AND THE FAST OF IT

NATHALIE STEPHENS

THE SORROW AND THE FAST OF IT

Nightboat Books / Cold Spring, New York / 2007

Tu as raison, nous sommes sans doute plusieurs et je ne suis pas si seul que je le dis parfois quand la plainte m'en est arrachée ou que je m'évertue encore à te séduire.
—Jacques Derrida

◻

It is possible to write one's day through letters, a letter.

Here in this city the letters are many and the days are many. The city that was to be every possible thing that came before. I admit I exalted it. Now there is the broken glass river and our cut up feet. Now there is a horizon of hydro lines. And bridges. From a distance they might be beautiful. But underfoot . . . There is a small island of herons. And just beyond the beginning hunting ground. Gunshots. The dogs madden. City dogs.

Their hearts furling. And me? I bark along with them.

I was looking for something to soften living. The collapse of it. The reach of it. It was a coldest winter. The river was not wistful as I had imagined it. Intempestif was the word I used. Wind billowing the rapids even whiter. Magisterial. I could live here I thought. Hook my eyes into frozen rock. What was I thinking? It is six months and already I am leaving. Eugène said une ville en vrac. He was right. What I first saw was monumental. A saillie of gorgeous concrete. Stairs spiralling. Turrets. A rue piétonne. Pigeons shitting on cobbled walks. A joie de vivre? It is best not to dream too much. The dogs began coughing. I laid down on the ground. Just to see. The police man moved me along.

Here there is one poem and the poets keep writing it.

There is a fever that overcomes.

The first time was summer and the dogs were delighted in water. The second was spring breaking. Both were evocative. A skin detaching from bone. And something scraping thinly between. It was madness even as it wasn't. There was a plank of wood and I laid my body on it. That became the city for falling. Bone was more breakable. And the fragility of it was unbearable. Duras would have termed : la femme. Am I wrong to contest? My sexe is limp for days. Even as my fingers.

A madness beginning at twelve. A bruising cough. And a sky turned yellow. The smell of change. An eradication. It isn't enough to have lived it. The liquid of the city running from my veins. The danger is in explaining. A book opens. The rest is fall.

The vocabulary of it is instructional. Skin splitting plainly along two sides of a fine blade. The blood is slow to come. When it does it stops at the surface. A fine line of red. When I think this way I encounter the absence of colour in language. A whitening on some surface. I took it for erasure. It wasn't. The whole city moved in that one direction. Funnelled into white. The shriek of it. Even the doomsday man fell silent. Vaulted. His hands studded together in prayer. When the dogs fell upon him I turned away.

Is it even plausible to speak of after?

The lure of Kossakovsky is the plainness.

In an hour I am leaving : Je m'en vais.

This is simply fictional. The leaving is return. The wind changes. It is always against. For the layperson such as myself this is one way to conceive of geography. As a series of currents changing always in the direction opposing the movement of the body. I have been accused of wistfulness. Of variation. Inside Calvino's book I encountered W.'s pilfering hands stealing lines into her.

Is this how one encounters oneself? Splayed infinitely across someone else's backside? The map is a toilet paper. Our desires are a strange dereliction. Seized upon. A book is not what it was. How could it be? That is nonetheless an insufficient argument against yearning. This square of grass dotted with the excrement of so many lying-down dogs. The sea is where I am headed but it is unimportant to name it.

From here nothing is possible. The leaving. The return. C. became the wind under the bridge, rushing, and no hands to catch him. Least of all mine. What am I to make of October? A month of many leaves. There is the sky over Guelph and it is discolouring. It is as it must be remembered. Funnelling a wide yawn into my mouth and a disturbance from my body. A heaviness in colour. And uncertainty. And sweep.

Unletter me. I said this underneath speaking. A long

thin pall of sound. Skin electric. Faintly. I would want to be manifold. The word can only ever be Buber's. And most likely I am using it wrong. Or inventively. Why not? Between here this roaring sound and the body that receives it is only the vestige of a certainty. Or worse a conviction ground down. Rejects it. There is a way to continue in dismantling. A further partitioning in remain. A repose in retreat. A sanctity in maim. None at all.

There is a way but I don't believe it. And you will not show me.

Bodypart. Letter by letter. Remove what's missing.

☐

A mark of singular unimportance.

I am retracing steps to the beginning. The artifice of motioning. This is as I madden : the food cart is a dog rushing at me. The road turns up faces. The sun drops into a lake suddenly and I am left standing. There is

bombing. And my pants keep falling down. The thing
with Norwich is that I am not here. I call the dog. I swal-
low a tear. I disavow the sky. The futility of conjecture
is such that I can only ever want. It is not so much the
wanting as the having been. None of it.

Here now. As though such a thing were possible.

To touch what is missing. Ce qui manque. I pull the
round white sun from water and muddy my feet walk-
ing in a circle. Circles around. The days begin with
ending. The wind is northerly. It is not so much grey
as it is colourless. And so I wear orange for balance.
But none of this is relevant. The strangeness of circles.
Their roundness and their emptiness. My hands push
through to nothing. This is the thing with circles. Their
constant turning and me turning in them. If I mark a
spot X with intent to return it is very likely that I won't.
If I mark the same spot X with no intent to return it is

still very likely that I won't. Will have been. This is the thing with tenses. Their governance and the insolence of our lives. Say : What was. Will have been. I mark the spot X and rub the ground hard until the X disappears. It only disappears insofar as it is not visible to those who did not put it there. As for me, it is in me and I see it always and besides I needn't because it is there.

⬚

A withholding.

The first difficulty is location. The second removal. And the third, more cumbersome, persistence. The persistence of the thing not leaving. The thing pushed away that remains. The incessance of the variance of the stumble and fall touch splinter fail.

A tracing.

Marshland. So this is the River Yare. It not so much is as isn't. Moor hens, pampas, broad horses the colour of cows and boys pissing under a bridge. Not a sound.

A blight.

Not so much want as want not. In negation. The city that does not want remembering. The movement that does not want completing. The book that does not want writing. The body that is already open. Opened.

I will tell you : A room with a window. A small body. A smaller body still.

☐

Say to me : Nathanaël.

Say : Nathanaël this is the book I have written you. It is pages and pages of feigning sleep in order that you will come. Say : You will walk over moors to the window that opens to this room and you will enter cutting your hand on glass. In this way, I will know that you are real. And I will kiss it all over you until the blood is gone and there is nothing left but the smallest piece of glass on my tongue.

Say : You are the daughter and the son.

It is too much remembering.

So many words for hyperbole. So much emotion in extreme. Movement as though toward. For S. I would do anything. What anything?

Because the body made sense before breaking. Because the question didn't need asking. Because the mother was the first place and what came before was only relevant after. Because bastards ululate on Saint-Denis at midnight, moon or no moon. And I ululate with them. With my scarf tight around my throat, mamzer. And my dogs cowering because they don't like to see me like this. With my mouth wrapped around a sound, cabrón, I am incapable of making. And gestures that are too grand for my body. The city echoes every sound I make. Even when I am not speaking. That is the silence from which I fall. That is how the body cleaves and the accent tears from the tongue. I am forlorn and I am ghastly and I will write down all that I can't remember. Beginning with a name. The same name spoken twice. And it shatters on the ground.

And the glass on the sole of my shoe is proof of nothing.

□

I imagine many names. Idle names and names that erupt. A name that does not formulate corruption, a name that is as indecent, as effluvial, as touch. A name for the parts into which you disappear. For the sullen and the tragic. For the movement especially. A name for giving and removing. A name for every unessential thing. A name too burdensome for my tongue and the air rushing from my lungs. A name to whisper. A name, an utterance. Pulled up from this marsh. Round as the moon burning a white hole of light. My knees pressed into mud and the echo of hammered stone. Bloodrush to my temples. A name that is at once shatter and groan.

Tell me, is it possible to love without leaving?

In the rows of books you become visible. I have come to think of pathway as gangplank. And the step as vital. Insofar as it is motion toward fatality. The potential for ending.

Between the library and the flat, the lake is always behind me. I don't believe it. Because lettering is a conceit of inscription. In the small graveyard outside Cromer's cathedral, the stones are letterless. It was not possible to climb the tower stairs. We must carve deep. And distrust our knives (sharpened on stone). I hold mine in my teeth. It is grotesque to consider. So what am I to make of these rutted books? It is ignominy even to ask.

Nonetheless, I hold three memories of a horse eating apples on a beach : none of which I will divulge.

And the small pinch in my palm where my nail dug.

I had wanted a notion for movement. A way around naming. Or the justification for my inability (unwillingness?) to name. To write of writing is a disloyalty, a selfishness. It is also possible that a book is less the appearance of a self than the disappearance, a grievance against a self. To wit : This rotting apple. This wetted stone. And the North Sea surging out of me.

Who put it there? That particular shame?

☐

I hungered.

The long flight. The impatient hôtelier. A particular shoreline. And everywhere sheep. And they were bleating. I needed to go outre-mer. With the father. I hallucinated arrival.

(There is not a single you I can account for.)

I folded a whole length of body into the window. Light moved through me. It was fire. And the whole city ignited. A January such as this!

I was born in the midst of demolition. One July, church stones toppled and a few blocks away I came alive. It was a faithlessness, a knowing.

All of winter tunnelled into a dog's ear. He heard nothing but white from then on. And his eyes shone out. For the hush, the rush of winter. His wide paws padding over light.

As for me, I walked on the frozen river to where the ice was water again.

The madness was not a madness of disbelief but one of tracing.

There is the silence from which it is not possible to speak.

The silence not of death but of the body's immobility. Between winter and summer an entire season suspended. Here at the outermost edge of speech. Like this: a surge of sobs dilapidated an already swollen chest. A bruised tongue from holding back screaming. And a fine needle—finer—threading sound back into the skull through the forehead. It might have been a way to die.

From the outside inward. The whole face suspended inside an undelivered call. And so on through flesh toward bone into marrow. The place where silence lies. Unrest. Circles of bright white light behind the eyes. And gaping holes where vision was. Everything turned. The body on itself. And the hint of your voice, mine, obliterated.

A lettering, I said. But before that.

Language ignited the brain's synapses. Until spring didn't come. And the body tore itself upon the confused edge of ice whetted by flame.

It wasn't desire nor the memory of desire. But the absence of memory or its omniscience. A body overful of wanting to forget.

And this question : What do you see?

I anticipated everything save that very absence. It was both the absence that watered me. And my willingness to drown.

⬚

Shall I tell you my own becoming suicide? The bodies of water stake each their claim. I might say surge but tell me who is listening? The books are counted. The dogs have been fed. The cats poised on the windowsill.

The letter might read : Too great a distance.

Or : To want wanting.

The many futile letters. (Humans proliferate so glibly.)

This is as it is devised : To B., *The Art Lover*, with this caution : All those blackened stones.

Not a book, but what becomes of me. The suggestion of it. Pressed against paper that like skin will burn.

You will miss me Maman but what of it? There will be fewer arguments. And fewer interruptions.

⬚

One of us is wave. One of us is shore. It matters little which. A tempest is unfurled.

Position is against. Consider : the Bay of Biscay is to the French the golfe de Gascogne; to the españoles, el mar Cantábrico and to the Euskaldunak, Kantauri Itsasoa. (And so on.) Our languages are bridges splintering.

If madness is indeed an excess of remembrance, I have come to this embouchure to argue against remembering. To place body where river opens to sea. To offer bone to rock. To scale this moutainous topography. To embed stone in my feet. And chalk a path over hilltop to sudden cliffside and crevice. Among dogs picking through gravel skeletons.

Who of us is (truly) lost? There is a corpse on carrer Dagueria. (Remember it). An embattled traveller. In the métro Jean Macé, a woman twitches and screams. The problem is falsely posed. A line of blood runs through cobble to earth. The citizens are gawking.

How will you kill me?

I too want to be wrapped in yellow tape. Draped in blankets.

Some live by hyperbole.

⬚

Imagine a love threaded a red thread finely. Bodies on a bed lifted. Lengths of gauze. Lips offering bruise to hip exposed, clavicle, pubic bone. So much spilling. It is precisely this gesture of want, this manacled city, this unearthed sound, that falls hard against earth, scattering the dust of actual suffering. Don't you see? What pulled body to ground, what hastened lip to groin, raised ass to bone tenderly, haltingly, what screamed This night alone, what damned the fool who wanted me, what summoned the fierce call that beckoned echo to stone, drove sewage from the sea, forsook desire, wounded nothing, salvaged nothing, emptied what wanted emptying.

Touched me.

⬚

The cities fold over and over. Union Square shows up at the foot of Montjuïc. The Chicago River cuts a path across Dartmoor. And the Orio stops at the foot of St. Denis.

I wonder at this particular cruelty. When gazing out of Bilbao's Guggenheim at the Jardin des Tuileries. Steps from Division Street overlooking the North Sea.

We have bequeathed ourselves to a sinister geography.

Who might you be who broke so delicately?

We stand each at the edge of a river whispering. We are foraging for greatness in among strands of algae.

Who willed the body? Who sang its praises?

The letters travel across the city. Past a wooden door, up three steps to another door where you are prepared to receive.

Please. The city doesn't allow for such complicity. They have drowned in the gutters and sewers and I have drowned going after them. They are caught in my hair like so many impurities. And when the authorities find me, I am gluey and sticky, ink-stained and swollen. My organs are indiscernible from the letters they keep.

This is as you are able to identify me.

To have allowed entry to so many things.

The word fragility. A death. The many insufficiencies.

Tell me : The light in November.

Here might be the only place worth leaving.

Not without you I said. But the moment was gone. The river ran uphill and the fire brought the city down. I wanted heat. The distance was too great. Wasn't great enough.

Every possible sentence is incomplete.

None of the nameable cities remain.

There is everything to fear. In the silence that befalls the body. In the surrender of breath to the atmosphere.

Say : Stay. Say : It will turn over and over and move through you. You will drink water from mountains and you will open and you will be light and you will turn to where I lie holding the sounds that comprise you. Say : Nathanaël I walked this far to where you are.

You will love me before I walk out to sea.

The dogs will bark. The cats will raise their heads imperceptibly.

You will cough up a faint trace of blood into your handkerchief. And you will not weep.

The sky opens it always does. From here to the lake the

freshly born birds fall pink from all the standing trees. I open my arms to catch them and they break against me before breaking against concrete.

We all wanted to fly and flew groundward with the wind in our ears and the thundering rush a kind of absolution. Toward ending. And our spines shortened and we walked further and further from city to city and from sea to sea, crawling, drowning, our voices arrested deep in our pink throats unspeaking.

This is where you find me. Hungering. With your two hands you open the walls of my heart and find the skeletons of so many just-born birds. Their unopened eyes. Their veined bodies. Their stilled pulse all that might be left of morning.

The walls fall and the heart seizes and in this way we agree again and again to surrender. And there is no one to catch us. And the sky is pink raining dying birds. And who might we have been, as a species, had we caught them?

The dead warn copiously against love.

I spent the last of winter emptying sand from my shoes. From end to end of a single long shore interrupting the sea. Walking. As though cobble could account for grief. And my feet could subdue the sovereignty of retreat. It was a moment of many moments with my two arms swinging and my hands tied. The water ran over and sifted me. Weathered me. Until I became dark rock and the hard waters below. It was a whole edge of earth splintering. Where skin split runoff endangered me.

All the waters of the world run to the sea. To where the earth is comfortable and worn.

We wash the dirt from our hands. We are that cowardly.

Just as I was leaving.

The city dust fretting the street. It was a book of many fragilities. The sanctioned, the vilified, the meek. J. said an inhumanity. For the poised the poisoned the constancy. I wanted to touch what was underneath. To dislodge the body from performance, gesture from posture. To make the heart the first place. Before even the mother. Before even the sea.

It was the brother's voice came after me. The son of the mother. The brother of la fille. It was the book's spine splitting the weight of my fingers. It was the body's weight subtracted from the body's breach. A hollow hollowing. Sutured. Stuttering. A book marked folded. Smouldering.

It was unloved smothering. The small hands gathering spit sleet. The momentum of the thing coming at me. The many faced years pressed up hard against concrete. Night ground into me.

Whoever said Nathalie founded that trajectory. Threaded me l'aporie. Then said pointing an ugliness a discrepancy. A girlness unremedied.

It was sleep unsleeping. Edging body from earth. Mouth from an architecture of misery. The soft words from the soft place unheeded.

□

Say : Distance is only distance insofar as it displaces you. Desire as it broadens you. The wide pall of earth is an emptiness, a yearning. Listen for the call of the beasts. For the light pad over wood of animal feet.

Say : What sacrificed want for need weakened humanity.

□

Every distance is a walkable distance.

The city designed a body of conjecture. A body of seemingly. Took the splinter of grief and laid it alongside the iron railings, the steel spikes, the concrete reefs. Grafted that relief onto a sublimated geography. Made distance decisive, unmysteried. Pushed what was splayed in deep. Wanted for a certainty. A fantasy of free.

So walk with me. To the cut edge of winter. To the carved out memory of sleep. Set fire to the cities welling out of me.

We fashioned ourselves of genealogies. Of bloodshed. Falsified the familiar gesturings.

I will tell you : The thing kissed into me. The thing made the city unsightly.

Ran. Runs from me.

☐

The body foretold the city. Armoured what wanted armouring. Sucked a blue stone deep into a hidden cavity. Mined itself for gold. It wasn't so much what had as hadn't. And the stretch marks showed. What grew from the blue stone was ironclad. And never told.

Someone said rain it rained the earth was wet.

Isn't that what was said?

We were windswept, indiscreet. The street map pointed east so we wandered west. To cleft rock and the muted centuries. (The mutinous sentries.) We played like that with the whole damn alphabet. For the incensed, the senseless, the stupidities. Crying out all the time :
Breach!

We thought we had found breaking but broke instead into ourselves. Pillaged the greying handheld remains. Making light of dust. Saying we ruined the ruins laughingly.

Shall I tell you instead?

We walked to where the dead lay dying and turned our heads.

Must I defend the maddened against the maddening?

Truss the unruly legs of speech for the sanctity of the bindery. Touch what became unsheathed. The language of what is unspeakable. Unseen.

The body anticipates its own retreat. Furrows into the blood drained carcass. Opens itself along a thin edge of steel. Beckoning defeat. Something more wild. Less complete.

There is a savagery to telling. How the body becomes disorderly. What is held, then misled. The mother foresaw the first disgrace. From inside years of the same wounded tirade. Etched like this finely on the body's page. It is nothing worth reading. It is all the torn paper from all the worn books rutting the many bookshelves. It is all the cities burning. It is all the water running from all the mouths into the charcoaled streets. It is the very plague that surrenders grief to some implacable enemy.

So how will you guard against the frayed edge of sleep? The brother's breach? How will you love what· is unloved in the first place? Trace the blooded furrows to where the body has no need for names?

It is too much anticipating. The climb and then fall. The cut and then bleed. The hammer then cleave. The language then call.

What was madness was simply the sound of bones breaking. And the noise that buried them.

☐

Say to me : Nathanaël the thing I held in the palm of my hand. It was the play of light on water. It was the same stone buried twice. It was the drought and the waterfall. It was the dry desert of the mouth. And the knot of desire hardened at the groin. It was the body unfolded from its pain. It was the overgrown streets and the whole earth in rain.

Say to me again and again : Nathanaël you were not born into this. The wind came and I touched your name. Nathanaël. Again and again. Nothing remains.

☐

I hadn't intended for.

The thing coiled at the base of the spine.

I stand at the foot of Gordon Street and beckon the rivers to me. It is as close as I will get to remembering. But for the hollow on my tongue and the cleft in my chest. The heart grows a wilderness and the dogs roam freely. I offer them the impartiality of suffering. The throb of some memory beneath a plate of steel. A finely etched carving suffocating the body's ability to feel.

What then? Touch the place beside me. It is full of having been. That whole length of living. From the lake to O'Connor and no place between.

☐

Who do the wounded wound?

Who wanders a finite distance along a dark road up a steep hill to a rock jutting out to sea? Says : Steal into me. Wake me from sleep. Spill out of me.

The drowned are drowning here in this hemisphere. We've discontinued the waters for something less deep.

There is a symmetry of rutted and bleed. In this particular fantasy the train derails and we walk on. It is not so much a courage as it is an insistence. To touch what doesn't want touching. To maim ourselves any way we please.

Says : History girded me. Placed reinforced walls right in the middle of me. It was up and then over. And again and again. With a small knife in my teeth that I swallowed each time I fell. Where were you when the earth came at me? When the sweep of that particular dream left? I held your voice from the phone and the eight words you wrote. It was the many pages tearing. It was the many lines stopping. It was the many gardens stifled by the earth hardening. It was the swell of your organs against a particular memory. It was all the ways for leaving. And again and again. You might have caught me. It was up and then over. Every time I fell.

Doesn't say : Make me.

☐

The book began as a misgiving.

As an obstruction, albeit pliable. It was possible then to lean into it. To crease the unworn face and speak it from a particular sensorial fold. It was open even as it closed. It was a whole earth that wanted rescuing. And the waters that submerged.

What a place.

What goes in is one thing. But what came out hung on the way the jaws of little dogs do. So I hung on too.

What have I to show for it? Bookshelves lined with Celan, Kofman, Pizaranik. And a long white scar from breastplate to groin. It was the heart wanted bisecting. All that bile spilling out. It was the fingers wanted evidence of some soft bloody thing. The blade was rusted.

The wooden hilt came off in my hands. Not so much what washes off as washes under.

The day you arrived you placed your two hands against a pane of glass. For the light. For the viscosity. It might have gone something like that. Had it not been for the little dog's jaws and all that water.

Where the beasts run the skin folds over and over. It is what is wild to begin with, the fall of hooves, the shiver of the whole earth, the whole earth shivers, that certainty. And the question that follows. The sky unanswering and our dark eyes closing. What touches is less certain than the word set against it. Is a rush of water over land that migrates to the sea. Is the mind's inability to recall even the simplest of things. The mouth emptied of its names. A body unfolding. A voice demanding Surrender me. Body to mouth. Earth to atmosphere. It is all the ways in which we come apart. It is all the ways in which we agree to leave.

There is not enough night until morning. The blood gorged vessels open what is closed. The tightly fisted muscle loosens its hold. A surge of sound from the viscera.

We run our hands through the ravages. We touch the relic of a thing once whole. As though the hands in that thick liquid foraged a wildness that might yet be human, a substance that needn't yield to form, a heart, the shape of which is unknown.

Who wanted for that fantasy? For the command of what is fearsome forlorn. For the rending the rendering.

The place where we walk is already miseried and our feet heed the lament of the fragile ground.

You count the years leading away from me.

In adornment and philosophy. In rivers' edges and wrought bridges, rusted scaffolding.

Accuse me your city.

After the wide-angled sea. The tall pines felled. The stones where some sit. The waters seditiously.

Say : You but for the body fell against.

It is the same day.

It is the same day.

It is the mouth torn open on some seam.

I wandered inland. With the dogs uncomplaining. I turned my back to the sea and beckoned the land over-take me.

It was like this : a bookstand and a microphone. The day's sharp incision. The body draining. Un livre.

It was the man's need to speak. The impatient necks craning. The again and again of speech.

I listened for the many doors closing. The heart's sud-den seizure. The compression of centuries into one solid moment of bereavement. The thing that I touched did not weep. The body did not fall in the street. And the man went on speaking.

No one said : Nathanaël fold into me.

Nor : What we destroyed of history we redeemed with inscription. The hand holds what is wounded in offering to some dream.

I turned the page and tore it.

The beasts shook their heads and showed their teeth.

Twice winter came.

The shadows shortened and then shortened again. Our bodies grew thin and our mouths kissed what was unnameable. We touched with our hands every place we had been.

The sky became stone and the city fell to ruin. The people drowned in their tears and the earth stank of urine.

The voice that rose in song broke what was left of speaking. What promises had been made became dust. What consolation unbelieving. The mouth stuttered and the ground with it.

We could not say What was. Nor Might have been.

It was every day ending and no way of telling.

The books later said we were forlorn. But it was different than that. We had seen our way to the heart's hard bone and broken it.

◻

Touch what is left of leaving.

Lift the torn edge of sleep and swallow what is missing. The river spills we weaken. The bedsheet tears we are naked. The lines of glass score our soft palms there is little left of meaning. Not the cold ground. Nor this shameless idolatry. We speak. We are spoken. The call hollows the heart stalls the wild summons.

Come for me.

I went to Hell.

It was the same city all over again. It was the same scurveyed sun and the people milling. There was talk of sacrilege and a voice demanding. The street map buckled. It was all in good fun.

I walked to where the road caved. The little girl pulled her pants down. A goat died and we drank its blood. The buildings were jewelled and the signs read Slaughter.

I for one went missing.

We both died. We hadn't foresight enough to run.

The letters go unanswered.

I take nothing of what is offered. Call it massacre.

This is the city demeaned. This is the city of set jaws and gritted teeth. It is the inscription of senility in bulges of fat and the remnant of broken schemes. It culls the weary from the defeated. It promises keep. It profers greed. It lifts the head toward expectancy. It grinds hard the knees.

I translate its deficiency. I call the mother's name out from under. I grope toward the sister she becomes illusory. I wear the mark of the city's architecture. I take the lover into the mouth. What becomes of me is scrawl is illegible is hollow is gloat is secede.

I open what is closed. I scream and I scream.

☐

The madness scores the skin. We balk at it before taking it in. We remove what covers. We are loathe to begin.

We solicit leaving. Shun the evening. The turn of the orange sun. The encroachment of what darkens. We fall fast. We bargain with our pain. We deny the thing that moves through dusk into the body. The ink-swell of rage bottomed into a flat plane of sufferance. Even our vocabulary is wrought of disdain. And the voices rise against us. And the hands admonish the thing we refuse to touch. And the body ignites the sorrow drowned in us. And the mouth starves the motioning of language. And the skin scars the having lost. Accuse the song named after us.

We are the unburied. And distrust.

I fancied myself the vestiges.

I worried the blemished turn of page with my rubbed fingers. I wandered the secular age with fury. I was indecent and carried stone like Moses. I was indignant. My bounded rage suited me. I pounded the hearts of many and disowned what I suffused with glory. I danced voluminously and made wet the sea.

It was a copious rendering. It was up and then under. The city-rock trembling. The sententious. The free.

⬚

Is this as we are? Is this as we imagine ourselves to be?

No one said : Who were you Nathanaël? Who stroked the body of the man. Who touched the earth and vanished. That same sad and wondrous. That same deleterious.

The book became of me. What we meant was overseen.

⬚

It could have been anywhere.

It was the book of the boy many times misplaced. Not what we thought. Nor what fell so quickly out of favour.

I will tell you : Just this once. The books that needed reading. The night heat. And a white light through a curtained window. Soft wood and a back coiled collecting. June, for example. And a green shelf lined from full to empty.

I walked all those days with my head against the ground. I walked a fine pencil line scattering the mysteries of my forked palms and my cut-out tongue. It was the voices of the many countries tangled into one. It was the spat-up city-block. It was the skinny buildings leaned up against the rotted sun. It was the meagre rations for the many-times won. It was the thing that consumed. The thing that was consummately undone. Tied like that into innards from the simplest of knots.

I could name them. The streets for beginning. The streets for grief and the streets for other times. From this window and the small collection of locusts wrapped in wire at my feet.

Don't you see? The daughters unwound from the book? The mother hung downward from trees?

All the grasses grow out of a fear. So we tread there and only there.

⬚

The footsteps retrace before being begun. The back turns, the buildings burn into an abstract sum. The crossed line is impermeable. I think it. Visible and invisible, a particular pull of sound, a magnificent aberration, a succession of any one thing, over and over.

I don't settle but fall. Contrive to fall. Against rock or oblivion. This is no way to ask a question. No way to unmake a wall. This is an architecture of bricked windows and strained pine. Of furrow and forestall. Tar paper gutters and limestone thresholds. Copper leaf lovers set in glass that doesn't shatter.

I said swamp. I didn't say mountain. It was a slip of the tongue. I turned right at the lake instead of continuing straight on.

⬚

I strip myself of this name. I turn from the shallow edge

of water to the only place. From the sandblasted city monument. From the uprisen cinder block. From the rat-trodden alleyways. To the vacant lot. To the stuck page. To the upended quarry. To the disheveled waterway. To the wasted days.

It is in the heaviness. The absent horizon. A steep climb of rock making the pulled apart mark for insisting, having insisted. The need for an other thing. A dry kiss in morning. What is left of the slept self clung to in fists that knot one indistinction to another. These are the designs of many unlovable gods, a knack for disappearance. A belief that can only be proletarian.

This might be the seizure of a desperation. The distance between lectern and slave. (Salve!)

It wasn't in answer to any one question. Rather the impervious feed of seduction. We are the most earnest of arrivistes. Seeking bedrock. Flooding instead in heat.

Our beds spread and every kind of love drains into the manicured field.

Tell me anyway : Your own harrowed retreat.

☐

Binds me.

No one said : Nathanaël you are what remains. Of the burst dream and the lake that drowned it.

Nor : A trace made in the place of this that is unmake-able.

We speak to be spoken. Or not at all.

☐

There is in the moment before the afterthought already forming. The footworn step, up and up, disappearing. A way toward reinvention. A stupidity no doubt. From Tibidabo to the sea a naked man lies then rises then lies again. There is nonetheless the fact of all that concrete between and a blue notebook abandoned in the sheets.

The many attempts at circumference. In the paper scrawl. In the unfolded map. In the trial then retreat. To speak of February in August replete. A plant that doesn't grow from seed. A stem that is rotted in flesh. The illogic of growth under a sky that heaves.

On an edge of water there is the thing and it is just out of reach. The man lies and so should we. For the impression made at the moment of leaving. For the city squares folded into the beach. For the rest of us who know nothing of the sea's voracity.

No one goes there. And why should we?

It is the same wrecked reason. It is the same imperfect measure. It is the same bored location. From window to ground. From body to wonder. From wall to whereabouts.

If it were possible we would stop. Wouldn't we?

⬚

It is this moment freed of itself.

I take the walking book from the shelf and set it on the ground. I squander that immediacy. This is as I dispense this particular remembrance. Who's to say? It collects in the hipbone on drenched days. It locks the soft parts into starvation. The throat lurches into the mouth and seizes up. So I swallow it into me.

I drink water from a rusted cup.

I rain with the sky.

I rain dust.

⬚

Nails me to this unnamable.

Not a theology of place. Not a masking of remembrance. Not a fortitude. Nothing as disabled, as damaged, as that. We wish for.

The significances fall each to the ground. The promontory ruins. The leaning bicycle. The chafed walls. The painted rooftops. The feral sky (blue, and blue). All of which might be liminal. A littoral. Won by water. Gagné. Verging and caught up. A wildness in a city corridor. A blank. A fill. An unwalled. A failed language in the place of a language that fails.

The awareness of a non-existent thing. The readiness with which.

In the other book. The book for waiting. The book for what is lost in the lost place.

It is the foreignness of the word please in a mouth that closes. In a mouth that masticates. Is the foreignness.

Isn't me.

We walk beside.

Here there is the second time. Here there is the unsaid. Here the altercation. After. It isn't easy like this to make a tracing of an unrecorded. Of a next thing.

I find a way to say. In multiplied passagings. The country of abandonment. The river of wreckage. The lines and lines for retrieving. The many forwardings. Like this undressing myself in a public place. The doors flung open. The oceans unabated. Rising a wall a wall rising an immediacy of counter and restrain. A doubt that widens into a body larger than every other body and it presses down and it makes everything small that was big to begin with in the very middle of what is intended to be wrong.

We didn't say : We will try again.

Nor : Ask me instead.

Try as we might we rise and we rise. The whole of everything beneath us.

Now there is a sadness.

(Is it good to say : Is a sadness ?) It is in the distance between the spent place. In the hill that would be la colline. In the mouth that says awkwardly prosim. A rail line crossing a bordered ground. The hands circling around a shared flame. The sadness that might be in the curvature of l'anse. What is cove. What is coveted. Covered. What a folded skin makes of scar. A rivulet for cut. A deep rut. And this is its outpouring. This is its gut. All pustule. All magotted and fussed.

An ended thing. Looked up.

I warn the masterpiece against its bigotry. I warn the beast against a verge of ville. I make myself flat in a field for wintering. I score the crossed-out text for lack. I lead the human to its walled-in dream. I claim a fake history.

I show my skin off. I eat colourful things. I make the light dim. I watch from a sealed window.

The mouth is in ruin. The words are copied out a hundred times. I make the chalk mark on the sidewalk in three differences. I do the other time. I stall on an underside.

Say aloud this time : We are as ugly as we mean to be.

□

Where have we been?

There is the waiting which must be mentioned. On a step up. Beneath an archway. It is possible like this to be triumphant. With a burnt flag for simplicity.

I wander toward a magnitude. This might make of deliberation a deliberate. A way of saying : Me voici. And : Laisse tranquille. The hand tired of caresses seeks a texture. Leaf, for example, or a ripple of rock. Or else deadening.

You reproach me the cities. Fair enough. But they have a way of being inhabited. Not because of vigor. There is the book's proclivity after all. And the redesign of this particular fatality. The fact of erosion. And what is made of edifice.

We build a house up in order to jump.

All the ways are lost ways.

It becomes very sudden. I wear a torn cloth. For the water place. For the lover's name. Who is also lost. Which is leaned into. With beasts who lean also. A precipice or meaning. Still, fall is fall. And what is given is a rent scrap of grieving. And it is this close to the thing we never saw.

I step aside for the bar of sound. It is a solid block and

elongated. Perforated with sounds that are disintegrated. In other words a refusal.

The fence rises around the tiniest plot of land. The body bricks itself into a shape. We are angled for the death watch. But what we look at is the worn surface of a tear. We see neither the water nor its transparency. We want lucidity and the tarmac. We want the surface ridded of its unpleasantries.

We want murder for headline. Dirt for grave.

☐

Aren't there enough of us?

There might be nothing left to imagine. Not a remnant even of a place. This collection of maps discredits me. The flattened out plane. The management of everywhere in a small wooden box piled high with books that are heavy. Fingers rummaging through to paper cut. A weight to temper the disgrace.

See to the memory of the unwelcome son. And the running daughters running. It begins like this in beginning. A beginning from a midway. A heart shrug. The hand raised to the chest accounts only for a small part of the thing. It is the startled pleasure of witnessed suffering. A desolation in the throat. In the throat.

With this knack for repositioning. With this want for having been. With this anger at the indirection. The thing reveals itself. The very place. But who am I to say don't or wouldn't for the other day.

I will tell you : The much travelled body. Pinned with four tacks to a peeling wall.

Adjust the unease. Breeze through a smokestack of praises and foment. Body curled up. Mouth inside a mouth. This is as we betray.

I say we for the many. I anticipate the dissent. To signify the gesture beside what isn't said. To disembark from this own failure. To point away. Here where it's written out. The despotic rounding of touched bodies.

The streets are unclean. It is every reason to lick the ground.

☐

I walk you toward a willingness.

This is how a road might bend : After Europe, the streets became straight. The traboules in exchange for the drive-through. The canals for Mickey Duck.

I take you in circles anyway. The disgorged river at your throat. Your mouth outpouring : Sea. A hand over every orifice. A hand over every place you might bleed.

You don't use the word regret. Discard it at every frontière. For the stone wall and the seam. For the pitted parts that secede. For the first time and the first time after that.

The country made the manner for leaving. It is the

thing you took for belief. A need to wretch after every
meal. To strip scar of skin and take the loose shards of
windows in deep.

☐

Say to me anyway : Nathanaël walk to where the river
empties into the sea. Say : Pick the stars from the sky.
Touch the stone wall that rises above you. Let the sea-
bed pull sobs from your feet.

Say : Go to the water. Go willingly.

☐

I notice a boundary around breathing. The dogs notice
it first in the sag of a half-eaten espalier. A garden grown
down into an earth that rejects it. I understand it as the
place where the head detaches. It doesn't hover so much
as soar. But this is inconsequential. What matter more
are the palpitations of the sleeping creatures for whom

there is no atmosphere. The green of the fabric on my arm is closest to sensuous. Without the ploughed follicle of dirt nor the abruptness. It was not the sea that parted but a plate of bone hafted to a screen of skin. The water passed and the light with it and someone wrote it on paper thin. The earth was framed and none could enter.

I am plying now the grimmest part of language. A stem made foremost for bending for binding. Tomes and tomes of liberty ill conceived.

This sentence then. How will you bear it?

Holds me to a ground.

The worst of it is incalculable. I perch on an indecision. The many parts collected and carried or else frayed to an indistinct contour. Either way they blur into the same liquid mass, appending.

I am tired now for the others. I read what is intellegible. I follow the faint trace into a hollowness. This is as I come upon an injury. An accommodation. An altered gait. We all have it. This particular way of walking over an uneven surface. The thing most uneven inside of us. For example a swelling in the palm. So what am I to make of offering?

□

We divide into occurrences.

A place name is an occurrence of retreat. A circle is an occurrence of light. A ground is an occurrence of destruction. A voice is an occurrence of a madness. A rail line an occurrence of parting. A boundary an occurrence of travail. A blood line of porosity. A chasm of pain. A literature of anxiety. A massacre of disavowal. A vein of rain.

This is the literal construction of the body. The body

in its built geography. This is how it is taken apart. And reassembled. The body which was to have been a body of ideas. A corporeal thought fleshed out on the rustiest of nails. We scraped away what was animal. We scraped away what was felt. We scraped away what was forgotten. We scraped away what was unexpected. We scraped and we scraped. To make the best of what could be made. We saw that it was glistening. We saw that it was smooth. We didn't see that it was tumid. And by the twenty-first century we didn't recognize it as rank. We gloried in superlatives. We split what was whole for the sake of it. Making from the made thing not thinking beyond the smoothness to the rasping breath.

Everything we made was for the next thing. Everything we made was rejected.

□

I line the closed mouth with an indiscretion. I line the plaster walls with sobriety. I enter the wooden doorway through a skin. I tear the asphalt from the limited. I pull the water up from the river and over a hill. I mark the iron gate inhabited. I go to where the beasts mourn. I place the key under the clay pot. I break the sleep of the disinterested. I lead the revolution to the bus stop. I burn the prayer that burnt the child tongue. I snap the clavicle from the skeleton.

I liken leaving to a photograph. With a spent bone in the tired hand.

I liken speaking to an epitaph. I drive the monster from the bedroom.

I wring the long neck. I carry the blue bruise. I tear the singed hair. I turn the blunt soil. I screw the turmoil. I call the city man. I turn his noise off. I follow the dog minstrel. I make the jerk off. I slam the mirrored door. I fake the sandstone. I wander the gravel dust. I snap the cello string. I swim the dry creek. I alter the sound wave. I float on the detritus. Among the shopping carts. In the boneless grave. I vomit on the plastic face. I humiliate the drunkard and the priest. I climb the spiked wall. I cross the poster out. I nail the infant to the fence. I line the people up. I proclaim a madness and a disgrace.

This is as the human breaks. Against the walled fortress. Against the lover's back. Inside the child throat. Under a beaming sky. Full of a shameless sun. Full of a thinning air of all the wars shunted into a stifled ground.

We eat it into us like cannibals.

⬜

There is the way to formulate an absence. In among the mottled sounds. In around the cramped formations of competing fears. The bodies press all into a window. There is neither light nor barrier and we neither fall nor are suspended. This is as we discover the structure and the structure chokes us into tight squares of paralysis. What I mean to say is the significance of gravity is lost to the body in among this many constructions. This is as we divine what we are on a verge of losing. This is as the sorrow is pinched into us. We hold breath against a hopelessness. We fabricate the disjunctures. And we swim across waters that are imagined toward lands that are devastated. For the fantasy of labyrinth. For the belief in astray. For the sake of gaining what is irremediable. For the hidden arteries releasing into a poisoned lake.

☐

I plant a garden in fall. I take the dry strands of withered plants. I pull the grasses from the edge of a lake. I make fistfuls of dirt and eat them into me. I make one garden inside and one garden outside. One for the body. One for the field. I pour water into dry earth. I take grown plants and make them small. I take old growths and divide them. I pull the sun close. I make the water fall. I press my feet bare against exposed roots. I cover the dry earth with wilted petals. I make the brittle stalks into a small enclosure. I call it an espalier an awning a canopy a stable. Even as it is none of these. Even as the hooves of beasts don't fall. Even as wood doesn't climb. Even as the shadow on the ground is the sky's own alone. Even as the garden is a slab of beaten rock. And the only sound is of a wailing cat on a threshold demanding a different course of time.

☐

I like nothing of what I see.

I close the door. I close the door for certainty. But the wall is weak. So I fall against the fallen wall on a dis-couraged ground.

It is like this : A sky remaindering.

In the museum of art there is a steel ring. In the river floats a silver box. Under the hood of a car there is a cattle prod. In a field there is a lead pipe. On a table top a monkey wrench. In this human hand an animal gut. These are the offerings. These are the settlements. These are the measurements of trust. These are the managings

that break and break and break us into madnesses. That make the surface into rust and the weaknesses for failing.

The ground is not for any of us. Not now that we have touched it.

□

It is the same season broken from the dog. It is the same season drained out of me. From standing. From sitting. Even from lying down. Is not the same as collectively. I walk the letter over this terrain and it befriends me. I ask unabashedly what overturns in meaning, in meeting, in modification. It : the letter or terrain. I take the human hand and wipe it all over me. This now is the value of secretion. Blood that is blood is the red

of blood not beet nor autumn nor cherry. The smell
of it. This kitchen window. This sweating back. This
entered mouth. The taste of it. In the most hated part
of the body. In the centremost part of the garden. In
the mimicry of empathy. Already you forget. And I. I
want none of it.

I say that I will speak for us. I say this and I am offended.
For you I am offended. I describe a loneliness. I call it
a solitude. I push a body into earth. I call it sensuous. I
make fire of all this dust. I choke it back. It enters me.
I pull a stone up. I call it offering. I fill the sea full of
stones until it walks under me. I gasp for the foreigner.
I ask the foreigner to join me. I call this peace. I call
this melancholy. I point to where the noises fall against
me. I point to the cows in their stalls. I say beachhead.
I point to the millions of stars. I say bullring. I carry a
knife blade to the abbey. I shore up the front step with
the wool of many sheep. I say tile for imprison. I say

languor for pain. I say molded for dreadful. I say tooth for name. I point to the lines of streets. I call each one a river. I say : Swim with me.

Now you say one thing only.

Now you say that I am mad. There is this way that you say it. You say Mad with it. I admit yes. Now that I am mad.

I am mad with it.

□

I turn the letters out.

Behind me are the cities and the vagaries attached to them. Now I speak of nothing. Now I pull the age apart. The age of lettering. I say a despot. I say considering. I say le chien claudique is true of all of us. I take the memory and make it ubiquitous. I call upon the trusted friend. I say the fire dust. I make the mockery. I make it very tall. For the leaning fence. For the pedigree.

I say in effect. I say for sense. I mean a dystrophy. But the mouth speaks for alleviate. I fail to find. The hand aflame holds the place.

Wait here. We wait.

☐

The last day claims all the days to come.

Now there is the parody. Now there is the upshot. I cling to the eventual concordance. And why not? The geographers claim each a succession. I demand an immediacy. It is this aporetic phrasure mimicking a solidity. A footfall that might be definitive that might wander without aim. A body a body. For the sake then of linearity : the mother the daughters the sundry. There is discord and there is the distrusted material. The book might have been sculptural. Then what? I might have thrown it to the sea. Instead it burns through the fingers the indiscriminate leaves. Turn. I turn. For what? The revival is measured and so inconsequential. This grain of sand, however disconcerting, is heir to our apathy and the bones that make for standing are the mismanaged soliloquy of thousands unrecognizable in form or sympathy. Want that is loathing. Touch that is occluded. For the betterment of suffering. For the wished upon and the filament of greed.

Listen. Nathanaël has washed his hands of me. Now there is the smell of smut decomposing. This road block. This fantasy that immures the better part of city. Bone for the sake of bone. Winter for the sake of removal. And for what a name?

The signs lose me my way.

I open the burnt book to the last page. I nail a single board across a window pane. I push the human in and out again. The guards embrace their prisoners. The crosswalks yield fresh passengers. The structures balk at being made.

The map announces none of this. Not the sunken marsh. Nor the bulleted stone. Not the fields of tar. Nor the wires exposed. Not the bodies that hang like slaughtered goats from tethered vines spouting sump onto the hillside.

☐

I give the thing away. I am certain I misplace it. The thing that wants ending holds the part that escapes. I make a summary of what remains. I say it once and then say it again.

The blood comes out of the mouth and the accompanying sound is abysmal. I want to say of it that it is phenomenal. Both the misplacement and the sanguinary. But it is other than this. What enters through the mouth corrupts what salvage might achieve of body. Exit is just as incomplete.

We stand in many doorways at once. We hold the sound and the memory of the sound and we arrive at neither.

Everything that was said said otherwise. So we walk in the undisclosed direction and beat our fists against the uncertainties that drive us. The armies arrive and we are relieved. We have no use for exoneration. And anyway the door is stuck.

I go to the middle ground. For the sake of having been. To find a better wording. The walls are made of glass and it is just as I imagine it to be. De glace I say. I say disfiguring. It is not a sharp place. Not as one might think. The hallways the runways the sideways are all empty. And I am hungry. So I walk to where the beasts lie and beg they eat what's left of me.

Not given nor forgiven.

For example. The reason determined the solipsism. The

heart of Pascal was a bloody mess and Weil saw to it that we should have none. As for me I blame the machine, never mind the hand that operates it. It is a convenient ruse. Now morality gushes from shallow cups. It is plain enough to see that the road is for walking and the river for washing up. Place may very well be the first false-hood. The second, more grave, may have been remains. For now it is good to have belief in the landscape. It too is fragmentary. We are all distant cousins of the square tile. Before asbestos. We too are friable.

There is a gravity and there is the understate. So I quit the monologue. The charges and the shortage. You claim it for posterity. Whatever it is outlasts us. Now we are catalogued into small cubicles. Scattered with pow-der. The language of it is removable. Dust, dust.

The fast of it is objectionable.

Now there is the lover. Now there is the friend. I might claim a disinterest, incredulity. If it weren't for the box crammed full of boarding passes. The paper wedged in the floor boards. And the baying dog baying. I blame the thing for leading me here in the first place. I make the distinction. Between the lover and the disgrace. I say it is the fault of no one. I hold the mirrors up. And the tape. I say it is the fault of everyone. I kiss it hard.

I make the same mistake. The snow falls just as heavily into the ocean as into the sea. We dive into the avalanche. We say that we are gaining. That the mountain is the part of us that damages our grief. I turn it over once and then once more. On the shoulder of the road is the beleaguered bit of us. We don't agree.

The sense of it might supplant. The painted pressed and flourish. For example the window is made of glass. The wall is made of stone. The ground is very hard. We run. We roam. We run. We roam. The senses make of me. The fragility. Brittled. Rapt. Turning.

Is a weakness.

I say sororale for the sake of descendency. But it is other than I intend it to be. At this border crossing the abomination is laid out flat for all to see. We spit gob into the palms of upturned hands. We wipe the expectoration onto the seat. We speak the language denied the many. We take the clothes from the body. And break the hips away from decency.

I don't make it as far as you. I don't arrive. I don't leave. I catch in the mouth of a memory. Now there is the dream without waking. Now there are the rows and rows of teeth. And the spectacle we make of me. The door on a hinge abrading. The elevator stopped between floors. The wood rotted into particles. And the fall of course against some hard thing. So I argue for the protectorate. What else can I do? The border is such that either way I cannot cross it. And here, on either side, does not exist. So I run headlong into it, partitioning.

□

I seek an evidence that is tangential and seductive. I have fear for my kind and greater fear for the rest of everything. Kind without a kindness. Now it is reductive to speak either of autonomy or a bind. The madness disallows this. And the question : Where might I be. It stops short of a possible trajectory. It wants possesion in the place of history. It anchors to ancestry and the manipulations of speech. It wants more than it can give and so gives it away.

I stand on the roof of a building that is condemned. The walls lean and I lean with them. We wait for collapse. And when it doesn't come we tear it down instead. We say no to the part that trembles. And hammer it to bits.

☐

You think to think me and then I am gone. You cut the letter from the paper. You peel the plastic from the glass. You pick the pattern from the surface. You score the grain into the passage. You close the throat against the sound. You fill the holes full of keys. You determine the peripheral. You raise the masonry to trowel. You bow the horse's head. You stir the water in the cistern. You consume the slaughtered fowl. You wear the feather at the groin. You say The leaf displeases me. You wear it down. You tip the boat into the river. Two by two sadistically. You catch the illness with impunity. You send the waste by letterpost. You shiver for the animal. You claim a fallacy for the body. You claim a nationhood as a prank. You take the parcels of land and fasten them to a yoke. The citymen claim unfounded. The hairy beasts enraged. The blood in the ground water. The shit in the downspout. The particulate inflames the membrane. The severance of the untold from the diatribe that might enable. Were it not for the part that breaks into histories that are inarticulable. You take the measurements anyway. You write them down. Years from now they are the gibberish for a system of believing. The feather-clad nomad drinking water from cups that face down on ridges of concrete edging some polluted swamp. We claim the antecedent. We organize into lines. We draw the proof from the blood. We fancy ourselves divine.

I don't believe you nor anyone.

It is a simple diversion. This propensity for survival. This insistence on the fixity of things. However porous the material. However drenched the surface. We describe our habitat in terms of nearness. A distance traversed. A distance witheld. Self as proximity. This is as we preach the geographies.

I tire of the city and myself in it. The city that made a desire of me. The city that poured the foundation for mourning. The city that is risen from fields river desert. That tumbles over bridges and sleeps in deep beds of regret. Doesn't recognize me.

Don't you see? We call out the name for the sake of our own voices echoing. We imagine ourselves reverberant but we are the thing that needs removing. We are the part that recedes from good sense. The sense of the senses. The sense of the senseless. And they are nameless. And they might be free. But they all smell of death. And they are tracking me.

The form bespeaks the formless. The mind the minor.

I make myself a messenger. I break the seal that cleaves boredom to the domestic. It is like this : The sameness of loving. Lettertorn. Florid. Seething.

The sister takes an orange stone out of the desert. The mother seduces the thief. I sit in the cubicle laughing. I look up at the ceiling. The ceiling falls in on me.

Now there is the laughter laughing. Now there is the ridicule belittling. Now there is the thought that accompanied. Caught in a scrap of metal that shakes with the shaking building.

I think nothing of it.

Still, what suicide begat me? What misery made to conceive. I pull at the knowledge of the bodies. Bodies because there are many. I grow from the memory of places. I grow from the refusal to the legacy. Between here this hand closed in teeth and here this lungful of seawater, the headrush headlong into longing and the anguish replete.

I could draw them out very simply. Here this riverside : a drowning. Here this rooftop : a nakedness. Here this admonishment : a particular accent. Here this tablature : a stony silence.

It might sound like this : Notes pounded out of a harpsichord. A scream welded to a bedpost. An insistent finger wagging. A head shaking its thoughts out onto the floor. Piss marking up the baseboards.

We forgive the ground for existing. We don't think to think of the furniture.

□

I build a house of mud and the ground up bones of animals. I fill it full of leaves and understanding. The roof is a probability. The latch is from another country. I stand in the doorway and the people come who remember me. The wind that rattles the skeletons is from a border town. The sun in the eaves is from a winter north of here. And the talk is a peculiar formality. What persists is the determined instruction of desire. The body of a memory.

Now there is the exhaustion in the limbs the language. Now it falters beneath the weight of the thing held up. The thing moved gently over the tongue and swallowed thickly into the throat. The thing knotted at the sternum. Rested against two bones pulled in twice as many directions. There is what is eroded and what is fractured. There is what is pulverised and what is shattered. In each of which persists some recognisable form or scent. Tooth or nail shred or remain rotted battered. An eye looks out onto everything. Catches the dimmest light and pours it heavily over an imagined place tracing many furrows into the skin pulled taut over some compromised surface. Plated filigreed maimed.

One step alone beyond an edge. Taken again and again. Into the body that absolves itself of walking and thirst. And the voice of the lover and the dull ache in the skull and the faint mutterings of the sorrow's porosity and the intransigence of rust.

□

I doubt the familiarity of it. Which is to say I cannot possibly. I take note of the unlikelihood. The heart turned out of its heart place. The boyhood the girl-hood the commonplace. I harden anyway. In the midst of the missive. I concede neither the humiliation nor the tenderness. Just the fact of entering. And the eventuality of a listener. I speak to the rivers. All of them. And run them through me. The water hole widens and disappears. What remains is not the trace but its concealment.

There is no telling. Specifically the indecencies. Not for reasons of exposition nor intolerance but for lack of intersection. At Hele Cross the mist dissimulates the cavalry. Dusk comes at morning. And so to walk is to walk in darkness. To swim is to be impervious. To stand is to be immured in a fantasy of chivalry. The body begins bodiless. But this is no reason to discredit its sufferings. Nor run it headlong into pity. The sleep competes with the sorrow. We cannot now afford discrepancy. Nor fall prey to the ideology of awakening. There are carcasses in wait.

There is nowhere to go. I speak to the premonition but it is of no use to me. I pick the river for drowning. I pick the swamp for asphyxiating. But the sky from the rooftop is dazzling and broad. Skies such as I have never seen. I board the plane for futility. The train rolls off its tracks. I make a walking path alongside the down-trodden. I excoriate the majority for stripping me even of this pleasure, this particular way of dying. What C. saw was indisputable. What city coveted was forlorn. What the mother turned from the doorstep. What the daughter ate into her head. What the miles and miles of smothering turned softly into the deathbed. Death not for dying but for the emptied out desire to feel a thing other than dreaded than miserly than sumptuous than sickly than ill-fed. Choked into me. Choked. Choked into me. Faulted.

☐

This is as it is displayed. In the angled hips of grown boys. In the dirt tracked onto a floor from outside. The management of thresholds is an arduous practice. Take the sexes for example. Their design is elliptical. The violation is foregone. So go the histories. It could have been you just as easily. Besides which the human is happily unaccountable. I promise nothing of the sort.

Not the freedoms of gestures denied. Not the niceties of consequence. When we go to speak only one of us survives. All of which is predicated on a gross miscalculation of distances.

□

I sleep through the agony. Mine and everyone's. This is no manifestation against any one thing, not coitus nor abstinence, but a caution nonetheless. Did not the death of the author precede the death of all things? Hélas, non. The cities are recklessly inhabited. Every aspect of which is mounted and derided. When I crossed the road into traffic it was a decisive moment for history. The compressed mess of steel that ensued was a symbol of this dark age, was a portend in metal obfuscating the obvious errors. When Dante wandered his way along the hot path, what he saw was inimitable, but this does nothing to preserve him from worship. The species has been unrepentantly foregrounded. Its animality suspended. The monument is overstated. We are left with shame and conspiracy.

I take my leave of the sentence. I book a room in a dormitory. It is not a room but the facsimile of a room. Between the sink and the window, the bed, and it is half as wide as expected, so the bodies lie folded sharply over an edge. And the screams and the cries and the smothered laughters and dressings and undressings and belches and ejaculate are discretely tucked into the strips of lathe protruding from the busted plaster. The layering of hands of skins of hands the insults the entrances gorge to bursting to billowing the pained and the pined for written out and disputed the phantasm the familial. It is this overlay that I wander. No evidence of its having ever existed, this very room, nor the landscape. Nor for that matter I. Believe me. I go to great lengths to rephrase it. It is this violence in the body transmitted to language overturned by the cities that exhort. And it is a particular way of speaking. And every justification for silence of a certain kind. For the mute call smothered out of existence.

□

I travel unaccompanied to the place where we meet. Even the meeting is an imagining. From Brnik I cross the river Besòs into the barrel chests of the douaniers. I declare all seven skins each of which sharpened against some indeterminate instrument. They brand a faint signature on my thigh and grant me passage.

What do I care? I lean across the bar and catch in the sigh of the casbah of the mother's memory. It vexes me. For this very reason I stay out of the homes of all the people. The yearning is a kind of innocence. But poisoned nonetheless.

What good to me is the shape of a body that cannot find comfort in the tenderest of places? All that is left is the unvisited. It too reeks of death and the poor habits of citizens. I go there anyway.

I howl at the city gates. I set fire to the doorposts. I watch it fall to ruin. I walk through the rubble. I say This is what it makes of us. I kiss Paris on the lips. I lie naked against Donostia. I stroke the ramparts of Ljubljana. I climb into Chicago's bed. I speak to the lover and the lover is dead. Dead in the city that tired the body of its walking. That tired the heart of its grieving. That lived in the place that collapsed under its own exhausted weight. That fell through falling to the unbidden to the foregone to the bludgeoned to the unloved to the desecrated to the livid.

Montréal . . . Chicago
(2003–2005)

ACKNOWLEDGMENTS

Parts of this work have previously appeared in *ars poetica*, *Verse*, *The Walrus Magazine*, *PRECIPICe*, *Melancholia's Tremulous Dreadlocks*, *Drunken Boat*, and the chapbook, *You But For the Body Fell Against* (Belladonna, 2005).

"An excess of remembrance" (p. 20) is from Shoshana Felman (*Writing and Madness*). And "the dust of actual suffering" (p. 21) is Foucault's as quoted by Felman in the same volume.

The author acknowledges the assistance of the Ontario Arts Council.

ONTARIO ARTS COUNCIL
CONSEIL DES ARTS DE L'ONTARIO

As for the many cities. They remain unnameable.

(To The Beasts)

To JM
    NS

ALSO BY NATHALIE STEPHENS

L'absence au lieu (Claude Cahun et le livre inouvert), 2007

Touch to Affliction, 2006

Je Nathanaël, 2006

L'injure, 2004

Paper City, 2003

Je Nathanaël, 2003

L'embrasure, 2002

All Boy, 2001

Somewhere Running, 2000

Underground, 1999

Colette m'entends-tu?, 1997

This Imagined Permanence, 1996

hivernale, 1995

ABOUT NIGHTBOAT BOOKS

Nightboat Books, a nonprofit organization, seeks to develop audiences for writers whose work resists convention and transcends boundaries. We publish books rich with poignancy, intelligence, and risk. Please visit our website at www.nightboat.org for more information about our publications.

NIGHTBOAT TITLES

The Lives of a Spirit/Glasstown:
Where Something Got Broken, Fanny Howe
ISBN 0-9767185-1-0

The Truant Lover, Juliet Patterson
Winner of the 2004 Nightboat Poetry Prize,
selected by Jean Valentine
ISBN 0-9767185-2-9

Radical Love: 5 Novels, Fanny Howe
ISBN 0-9767185-3-7

Glean, Joshua Kryah
Winner of the 2005 Nightboat Poetry Prize,
selected by Donald Revell
ISBN 0-9767185-4-5

FORTHCOMING TITLES

Sober Ghost: Selected Early Poems, Michael Burkard
December 2007

Your Body Figured, Douglas A. Martin
February 2008

In the Mode of Disappearance, Jonathan Weinert
Winner of the 2006 Nightboat Poetry Prize,
selected by Brenda Hillman
April 2008

Please order our titles through Small Press Distribution
(www.spdbooks.org).

Nightboat Books
Cold Spring, New York
www.nightboat.org

Library of Congress Cataloging-in-Publication Data

Stephens, Nathalie, 1970–
    The sorrow and the fast of it / Nathalie Stephens.
        p.   cm.
    ISBN 0-9767185-5-3 (978-0-9767185-5-0 : alk. paper)
    I. Title.
PR9199.3.S7839S67 2007
811'.54–dc22

                                                    2007021551

Original printing 2007.

Cover image: Jeff Marlin, *Untitled Drawing*, acrylic and graphite on
paper, 2005. Courtesy of the artist.